Legal and Ethical Implications of Social Media Practices

Table of Contents

We don't have a choice on whether we do social media, the question is how well we do it?

Chapter 1. Introduction

In this Special Report, we veer into the captivating, dynamic, yet undeniably complex realm of social media, uncovering its vast legal and ethical implications. Spanning from everyday user interactions to the strategies of multinational corporations, social media practices influence the world in which we live, work, and connect. We unfurl the full tapestry of this omnipresent modern phenomenon, highlighting how businesses maneuver within these spaces while respecting users' rights, privacy, and more. This report isn't just a deep dive into the complex mechanisms underlying our digital world, it's also a thrilling journey into the heart of the interconnected society we are part of. Your ticket to understanding this pivotal arena? Just a click away. Purchase this Special Report and immerse yourself in a detailed, insight-rich exploration of the legal and ethical facets of social media. It's a must-read for anyone aiming to navigate these digital landscapes safely and responsibly.

Chapter 2. Unveiling the Social Media Landscape

In this report, we embark upon the multifaceted domain of social media, exploring its vibrant intricacies, its transformational dynamics, and the colossal impact it has on our modern-day society.

2.1. The Evolution and Emergence of Social Media

Social media, as we know it presently, is a product of rapid technological advancement coupled with the innately human desire to communicate, connect, and share. Initially, the world was only privy to simple, standalone methods of online communication like emails and chatrooms. However, with time, these platforms evolved into more sophisticated communication systems that integrated multimedia, real-time updates, and multi-person interactions.

The first instance of such advancements came with the advent of social networking sites, such as LinkedIn in 2002, intended for professional interactions, and Facebook in 2004, initially for university connections which later expanded its reach globally. Since then, we have witnessed an explosion of similar platforms, each providing a unique way for users to communicate and express themselves, including the microblogging platform Twitter, the photo-sharing app Instagram, and the short video platform TikTok.

These social networks have fundamentally redefined the way people interact, shaping not just personal communication but also profoundly influencing aspects of society such as politics, business, education, and culture.

2.2. Defining Social Media: A Primer

Social media is a broad term that encapsulates various online platforms whereby users can create and share content, as well as interact with each other. These platforms often involve user-generated content, which means that the majority of the material comes from the users. They create, post, and react to their fellow users' posts.

Social media provides not just a communication channel for its users but also a platform for content creation and distribution, a source of news and information, a tool for marketing and branding, and a place where people can express themselves freely.

2.3. The Paradigms of Social Media Interactions

Social media interactions can be broadly categorized into three paradigms - I-to-I (Individual to Individual), I-to-M (Individual to Mass), and M-to-M (Mass to Mass).

In the I-to-I mode of communication, one person communicates with another. This could be through direct messages, or comments on a post. On the other hand, the I-to-M form of communication refers to content that an individual shares with a large audience, like posts, tweets, or videos. Lastly, the M-to-M interaction is crowd-sourced content where multiple users contributed to a particular content piece. This could be a Wikipedia page or a collaborative playlist on Spotify.

2.4. The Global Reach of Social Media

The proliferation of the internet and cheap data has brought about the democratization of information. Social media has played a critical role in this transformation, bringing people from diverse geographies and cultures onto one platform, facilitating the sharing of ideas and experiences in a way that was never before possible.

Statistically speaking, as of 2021, there are more than 4.2 billion active social media users worldwide, accounting for more than half of the global population. The global reach and influence of social media cannot be understated in this digital era.

2.5. The Profound Impact on Communication and Society

Social media has drastically changed how human beings communicate. It has altered the speed, scale, and even the style of communication. The advent of social media has seen vocabulary changes, the birth of social media-specific lingo, and the rise of a more visual form of communication with the use of emojis and memes.

On a societal level, social media has changed the way we consume news, how we form opinions, and even how we interact with our governments. On one hand, it has fostered civil discourse and empowered citizens by giving them a platform to voice their opinions. On the other, the misuse of these platforms has resulted in challenges like misinformation, privacy breaches, and cyberbullying, to name a few.

In conclusion, understanding the multifaceted landscape of social media is crucial to comprehend our continually evolving digital lives.

Like a sprawling metropolis, social media encourages diverse experiences, voices, and perspectives. This chapter has aimed to provide a rigorous, exhaustive, and thorough overview of the expansive social media landscape, setting the stage for subsequent, more specific explorations into the legal, ethical, and societal implications of social media. The journey ahead, much like the world of social media itself, promises to be intriguing, enlightening, and occasionally challenging – but always immensely rewarding.

Chapter 3. Legal Frameworks Governing Social Media

Social media is a domain that is briskly evolving, reaching new corners of the world every day, and finding innovative ways for people to communicate. It is essential to understand how rules, laws, and regulations govern it to ensure a fair and harmonious online atmosphere. This chapter sheds light on the legal frameworks that influence social media's functioning, enabling sectors ranging from ordinary users to massive corporations to navigate with clarity and confidence.

3.1. The Advent of Cyber Law

The emergence of internet technology has transformed our way of life, becoming an indispensable facet of our social and professional lives. In tandem with this rise, a novel area of law, cyber law, flourished. Cyber law is the legal structure that deals with the Internet's legal issues, including conflicts and problems associated with the usage of social media. It encompasses laws related to privacy, freedom of information, defamation, censorship, and intellectual property. Even though early internet users championed the concept of a 'free internet,' the wilderness of the online environment required order, leading to the dawn of cyber law.

3.2. Intersection of Social Media and Law

As social media platforms continually evolved, they became not just communication tools but also sites of business activities, information dissemination, entertainment, and personal expression. With this expanded role, the interaction between social media and various aspects of law has become more pronounced. In copyright law, rampant instances of intellectual property infringement had to be addressed. The data privacy law became essential with the massive amount of personal information being handled by social media platforms. Employment law also came into play as social media began to play roles in hiring processes and workplace behavior.

3.3. Privacy Laws and Social Media

When stepping into the discussion about privacy laws and social media, it is necessary to highlight the cornerstone legislation in this domain: the General Data Protection Regulation (GDPR) of the European Union came into effect in May 2018. GDPR mandates how companies - including social media platforms - handle, process, and store personal data of EU citizens. It solidified users' rights, such as the right to be forgotten and data portability, altering the power dynamics between social media platforms and their users.

In the United States, the California Consumer Privacy Act (CCPA) empowers Californians with similar personal data protection rights. Yet, the US still does not have a comprehensive national-level privacy law, leading to different practices across states.

However, privacy laws globally retain the same central idea – maintaining the rights and integrity of the individual in the vast digital landscape.

3.4. Copyright and Intellectual Property

Social media, teeming with shared photos, articles, music clips, and video content, naturally ventured into the copyright law domain. The Digital Millennium Copyright Act (DMCA) in the U.S., for example, provided a safe harbor for Internet Service Providers, including social media platforms, against copyright infringement lawsuits, as long as they respond adequately to takedown notices.

Globally, similar legal frameworks, such as the European Union's Copyright Directive, are being formulated and implemented. These laws not only ensure the protection of creators' rights but also try to reconcile these rights with the free flow of information and ideas.

3.5. Defamation Laws and Social Media

Defamation laws are especially relevant in the context of social media due to the ease with which damaging false information can be spread. In many jurisdictions, posts that defame individuals or organizations are considered unlawful. Still, the enforcement of such laws can be challenging given the global nature of social media platforms.

3.6. The Future of Legal Frameworks Governing Social Media

The aforementioned laws represent just a sample of existing legal frameworks that overlap with social media. As technology is constantly evolving, lawmakers are being challenged to keep up with emerging issues, such as deepfake content, AI-generated IP, cryptocurrency transactions, and more. This intensely dynamic interplay between law and social media indicates that our legal understanding and frameworks will continue evolving. However, these adaptations will and must always prioritize preserving the rights and privileges of all social media actors while enabling the exploration, expansion, and enhancement of their online experiences.

Chapter 4. A Deep Dive into Data Privacy and Protection

From the early, unsophisticated beginnings of social media, we've evolved into a dynamic and intricate digital landscape. This interconnected web of platforms forms an influential part of many individuals' lives, a crucial medium for communication, content sharing, and even business operations. However, with these changing dynamics come profound challenges associated with data privacy and protection. As we journey into this realm, we'll explore various facets, including user rights, legal stipulations, and protective measures around data privacy across digital platforms.

4.1. Understanding Data Privacy and the Importance of Protection

Data privacy, in its simplest form, refers to the right of an individual or entity to determine when, how, and to what extent their personal data may be shared with others. In the context of social media, this becomes particularly significant as these platforms become reservoirs of massive amounts of personal information. Users' names, locations, relationships, hobbies, interests, and many other factors are captured and stored, often becoming central to the commercial value for these platforms. Consequently, as more personal information is shared voluntarily or collected surreptitiously, the need for effective privacy controls and data protection measures is paramount.

4.2. Legal Aspects of Data Privacy

Regulations around data privacy vary considerably around the globe. Some nations, like the European Union with its General Data

Protection Regulation (GDPR), provide stringent guidelines for data privacy. These comprehensive regulations lay down clear parameters around user consent, data portability, the right to erasure and more, impacting international companies who interface with EU citizens. Across the Atlantic, the US approaches privacy through a sectoral model, yielding a patchwork of legal protections spanning several areas like health, financial, and children's privacy, but still leaving gaps in comprehensive data protection.

4.3. The Role of Social Media Platforms

The business models of social media platforms intertwine with data collection and usage. For these platforms, user data is often the key product, with detailed profiling enabling targeted advertising, personalized content, and other revenue-generating pursuits. Given this, platforms have a significant role to play in safeguarding personal data and ensuring adequate privacy protections. Developing robust privacy controls, engaging in transparent dialogue on data usage, and fast tracking responses to data breaches are some ways in which platforms can strive towards these objectives.

4.4. Privacy Policies: More Than Fine Print

Privacy policies form a critical weapon in the arsenal for data protection on social media platforms. These policies determine how user data is collected, stored, shared, and discarded, shaping the dynamics between platform and user. However, these policies often tend to be complex legal documents filled with jargon and legalese. Simplifying the language used, presenting information in digestible segments, and promoting awareness around these policies could greatly improve user understanding and allow for a more informed sharing of data.

4.5. The User's Role in Data Privacy

Individuals are not just passive recipients of data privacy practices but active agents who can establish boundaries around their data. Awareness of privacy controls on platforms, critical engagement with privacy policies, and judicious sharing of personal data are essential steps towards self-protection. Users can also leverage tools and resources available online to further secure themselves and learn about best practices.

4.6. Embracing Analytic Anonymization and Privacy Enhancing Technologies

Moving beyond the traditional approach of simple user consent, more proactive methods of safeguarding user data are gaining traction. These include anonymization, which involves removing personally identifiable information from data sets, and Privacy Enhancing Technologies (PETs) that help secure data transmission, storage, and access. These methods embrace privacy by design and offer promising avenues for progressing towards a safer digital realm.

4.7. Concluding Thoughts: The Future of Data Privacy and Protection on Social Media

The allure of social media is unlikely to wane in the near future. As these platforms continue to evolve, drawing in more users and branching out into new and innovative functionalities, challenges surrounding data privacy are expected to evolve as well. Striking a balance between the commercial imperatives of these platforms and the rights of the user is an ongoing task, and one of paramount importance in our digital age. The future, it appears, holds a continued need to push boundaries, innovate, and reiterate our commitment to the protection and respect of personal data, each step we take cementing our position in this dynamic digital landscape.

Chapter 5. Copyright Considerations in the Digital Space

Understanding copyright in the digital space, may initially seem akin to navigating a labyrinth, where each corner turned reveals a new, more intricate path that requires careful exploration. This chapter aims to elucidate this complexity, offering a detailed examination of copyright considerations integral to social media use and digital environments.

5.1. Understanding Copyright

Copyright law serves a simple, yet fundamental purpose: protecting original creative works and intellectual property. It provides the author, artist, musician, or creator, right to control how their content is used, copied, and distributed.

The advent of the internet and, more specifically, social media, has made the distribution and consumption of creative works effortless, largely benefiting society by making knowledge and entertainment readily accessible. However, the same ease equally invites misuse, allowing unlawful distribution, mimicry, or exploitation of content without the creator's permission. This is where the function and importance of copyright law becomes essential in creating a balance.

5.2. Missteps in the Digital Space

When considering copyright infringements, most think of the blatant transgressions—piracy, plagiarism, production clones. These are indeed part of the problem, but social media introduces more nuanced possibilities for infringement. How many of us think twice before reposting an image on Instagram or sharing a funny video on Facebook? Critically, these standard practices can infringe on copyright laws, depending on the copied content and its terms of use.

Being unaware of the laws doesn't absolve users from punishment. To be safe, it's preferable to know the scope and conditions of various social media platforms' terms of service, examine copyright licenses of content, and use only those images or materials permitted for reuse.

5.3. Copyright Law and User-Generated Content

The legal concerns complicate further with the rise of user-generated content (UGC), which is any form of content—blogs, videos, pictures, posts, etc., created by users rather than official content creators or brands.

Although UGC enhances engagement and encourages creativity, it also blurs copyright lines on who owns the digital content. It's a delicate terrain to maneuver on, requiring businesses and individuals to revisit their understanding of copyright laws and responsibilities in protecting rights, given this new paradigm.

5.4. Fair Use: A Silver Lining

Fair Use, under US copyright law, provides a level of flexibility, allowing limited use of copyrighted material without requiring permission from the rights holders. It's an essential doctrine, supporting freedom of expression by permitting unlicensed use of copyright-protected works in specific circumstances like criticism, teaching, scholarship, or research.

However, Fair Use's application isn't straightforward. Several factors are considered in these cases, including the work's nature, the purpose of use, the quantity used, and the impact on the market value of the work. These complexities necessitate a careful, discerning approach when handling copyrighted materials.

5.5. Copyright Policies of Social Media Platforms

Social media platforms, aware of their role in potential copyright infringements, have implemented robust policies to address this issue. Facebook provides 'Rights Manager', designed to help rights owners identify and manage their intellectual property on the platform. Instagram has a similar copyright policy, disabling accounts that repeatedly infringe others' rights.

5.6. The Way Forward

Navigating copyright in the digital space requires both an informed awareness of the law and a respect for the rights of content creators. In this rapidly evolving digital landscape, keeping abreast of changes is a necessity rather than a luxury, ensuring users and creators alike can protect their rights while contributing to the rich tapestry of content that social media platforms celebrate.

From the individual scrolling through their feed, the influencer marketing a brand, or the multinational corporation crafting a worldwide campaign, the call is to act responsibly. The onus is upon us all to uphold ethical practices in the realm of copyright as we move forward, engaging with and shaping the future of the digital world.

Chapter 6. Exploring Ethical Frontiers: Online Misinformation

The advent of the Internet age has revolutionized not only how people interact but also how information is disseminated worldwide. Online platforms have harnessed this power in remarkable ways, democratizing the flow of information and enlivening public discourse. However, this development has simultaneously given rise to a new, insidious form of communication—online misinformation.

6.1. The Emergence of Online Misinformation

Online misinformation is a pervasive problem that stems from the unregulated nature of the Internet. This form of wrong or misleading information is often disseminated under the guise of news, studies, or official reports, leading millions of users astray. Misinformation could be propagated either due to ill-intent or sheer ignorance. As suspected, the consequences can be as varied as they are devastating, tainting public opinion, undermining institutions, and distorting facts on matters of public interest.

6.2. Anatomy of Online Misinformation

Understanding the artistry of online misinformation involves a multifaceted immersion into its various building blocks. At the heart of these erroneous reports often lie convincingly distorted facts, fueled by embellished language and sensationalism. They are typically packaged with compelling headlines, aimed at hooking readers instantly. The proliferation of such falsehoods can be attributed to the speed and ease with which they can penetrate digital spaces, hopping from one user to another.

6.3. Ethical Concerns Associated with Online Misinformation

Online misinformation gives rise to several ethical dilemmas. Firstly, it raises questions about responsibility—who shoulders the blame when misinformation goes viral? Is it the platform, the user who shared it, or the originator of the information? Responsibility also pivots around the issue of checking misinformation. Should Internet users be expected to critically evaluate every piece of information they encounter online? Should scrutiny and fact-checking become part and parcel of online communication culture?

Secondly, online misinformation exposes the dangerous side of free speech, pushing societal discourse into territory that teeters on the brink of falsehood. Can the spread of misinformation be considered a form of free expression? If it can, where is the limit to such freedom drawn?

Thirdly, there are potential harms associated with online misinformation. The potency of online rumors can trigger public panics, political unrest, financial loss, and even harm to public health. It may also exacerbate social divisiveness or incite hatred and violence. Lastly, the proliferation of misinformation undermines the very principles of truth, trust, and transparency upon which the Internet was founded.

6.4. Legal Implications of Online Misinformation

Legal approaches to online misinformation vary across jurisdictions, reflecting differing cultural norms, political climates, and legal frameworks. In some countries, laws have been enacted to criminalize the deliberate dissemination of misinformation. However, these have been met with fervent debates around potential infringements of free speech and press freedoms.

Moreover, the interactive nature of digital platforms makes it nearly impossible for laws to effectively tackle this issue without interfering with the fast-paced, free-form nature of online interaction. Virtually anyone can be considered a publisher in the digital landscape, muddying the waters of legal liability.

This delicate balance forms a challenging ethical frontier, exploring whether the right to free speech should protect the spread of misinformation. Lawmakers and policy professionals continue to grapple with these issues, aiming to strike an equilibrium between protecting individuals' rights to access and share information whilst mitigating the risks posed by misinformation.

6.5. Towards Responsible Information Sharing: A Call to Action

The flood of misinformation underlines the need for a more ethically-conscious use and dissemination of information online. Everyone, from policy-makers to platform administrators and internet users, has a role to play in curtailing the spread of false information. Three guiding principles could serve to minimize the reach of misinformation: digital literacy, source evaluation, and proactive fact-checking.

In conclusion, as the digital space expands, ethical regulations must keep pace to affirmatively address the growing specter of online misinformation. The collective onus lies with us—a society of digital consumers and participants—to continually push for truth, rigorous fact-checking, and responsible handling of online information. As we navigate these turbulent waters, our compass should always point to a digitally literate and ethically aware society, steering our way toward a more trustworthy digital tomorrow.

Chapter 7. The Impact of Social Media on Employment Law

Social media, often celebrated as a tool for personal expression and communication, has also introduced a new dimension to employment law. The sense of distance encouraged by digital communications and the blended nature of personal and professional lives online pose fresh challenges to both employers and employees.

7.1. Understanding the Changing Employment Landscape

The world of work is not as it once was. Technological advancements, particularly the evolution and widespread adoption of social media, have significantly altered the nature of the employer-employee relationship. Employers now find themselves navigating through unprecedented legal and ethical dilemmas. These arise from questions about an employee's right to privacy, the extent of an employer's control over online conduct, and the boundaries between work and personal life-questions that until recently had barely existed.

7.2. The Double-Edged Sword of Technology

With social media providing ample opportunity for employment purposes, it can be a challenging landscape to traverse. On one hand, technology facilitates global connections and remote work more seamlessly than ever, making recruitment processes efficient and convenient. On the other hand, this multitude of online interactions generates a slew of legal issues-from discriminatory hiring practices to unjust terminations-that can pose significant legal pitfalls for the unsuspecting employer.

One such risk arises when employers use social networking sites to vet job candidates. While such actions provide revealing insights about potential employee's character and habits, they also expose employers to potential legal claims such as discrimination or privacy violation. Pre-employment social media screening can inadvertently open a Pandora's box of an applicant's protected class information. If a hiring decision is made based on this information (such as their race, religion, disability, or age), it could potentially lead to discrimination claims.

7.3. The Fight for Digital Privacy

Arguably, nowhere is this legal complexity more evident than in the realm of digital privacy. Employees often assume their off-duty online activities are private. But if those activities take place on an employer-provided device, or interfere with their employment obligations, the line of privacy can blur. Organizations maintaining a clear, comprehensive social media policy that balances employees' privacy rights with the need to maintain a respectful, productive work environment might navigate these concerns more efficiently.

The digital age continues to remold the legal landscape for privacy rights, forcing courts to regularly revisit the interpretation of these rights. Some countries, such as Germany, have introduced laws to safeguard employees from having their social media profiles scrutinized by potential or current employers. This clearly indicates the growing significance of privacy rights in employment law.

7.4. The Issue of Online Conduct and Reputation Management

Employees' online conduct can have significant consequences for the reputation of a business. Posts, comments, or shares, even on personal accounts, can sometimes have incredibly damaging repercussions for the employer's brand image. With the rise of the concept of "employee ambassadors" or "employee influencers", whereby employees are encouraged to share positive aspects of their work life on social media, these consequences can become even more significant. Employers can devise clear social media policies defining what is perceived as damaging online conduct, which could be a strategic decision to protect the business reputation.

7.5. Emerging Legal Frameworks

Even as social media morphs and evolves, legal frameworks designed to govern it struggle to keep up. Nevertheless, law-makers are striving to address these gaps. They are shaping laws that protect against discrimination, ensure privacy, and secure employment rights for the greater good. However, the balance is delicate; these laws must uphold the rights of employees without stymieing the potential of new technologies.

Overall, the impact of social media on employment law is profound and far-reaching, transforming both hiring practices and the maintenance of workplace culture. It warrants ongoing, robust discussions among employees, employers, and lawmakers. As society and technology continue to evolve in tandem, so will the legal sphere. This chapter is one step towards understanding these changes and facing the challenges of this digital era intelligently and ethically.

Chapter 8. Balancing Free Speech and Internet Censorship

The complex subject of balancing free speech and internet censorship unfolds within a landscape of diverse perspectives, contexts, and interpretations. It is pivotal to understand that this balance doesn't necessarily imply a binary or dichotomous relationship between free speech and internet censorship, but rather a symbiotic relationship where the existence and the magnitude of one often shapes the scope and relevance of the other.

8.1. Free Speech: The Cornerstone of Democratic Societies

Free speech stands as a quintessential human right, crucial to the operation of any democratic society. It provides space for individuals to express their opinions, beliefs, and ideas without fear of governmental reprisal. Nonetheless, the broad espousal and sanctity of free speech are not without their exceptions. Most nations are equipped with limitations on free speech, applied judiciously to mitigate instances of hate speech, incitement, defamation, and false news.

Internet, as a remarkable technological marvel, amplifies the potential of free speech by offering a platform that is, in essence, universal, instant, and anonymous. The seamlessness with which individuals can engage in discourse or express dissidence is both an asset and a challenge. On the one hand, it fosters a culture of openness and democratic dialogue, while on the other, it provides a refuge for those aiming to spew hate speech, propagate misinformation, or incite violence.

8.2. The Paradox of Internet Censorship

On the flip side of this coin lies internet censorship, a contentious exercise implemented often by governments and sometimes by private organizations or individuals, to regulate, restrict, or control the flow of information online. While its initial intent may be to protect societal harmony, ensure national security, or maintain public order, the broad ambit of internet censorship lends ample room for potential misuse.

Internet censorship can assume many forms, from the suppression of specific keywords, the blocking of certain websites, or the employment of surveillance technologies to track online activities. In many nations, restrictive internet laws are often cynically used to quiet dissent, suppress minorities, stifle journalism, and perpetuate authoritarian power. Herein lies a paradox: an instrument ostensibly for maintaining societal equilibrium can swiftly become a tool of overt control and silent oppression.

8.3. Striking the Balance: The Role of Legal Frameworks

Efforts to balance free speech and internet censorship are typically enshrined within legal frameworks. These can range from constitutional protections (where freedom of speech is explicitly referenced), legislative measures, or regulatory practices. The law, in this context, holds the responsibility of ensuring that the right to free speech is not unduly compromised, while also stipulating the boundaries where internet censorship is deemed necessary.

Creating such a lawful equilibrium is a daunting task. While free speech is universally espoused, its interpretation and implementation are contingent on the sociopolitical, cultural, religious, and historical context of a nation. Similarly, the legality and extent of internet censorship also differ vastly across the globe. Hence, while certain themes may be universal, the balancing act is often a uniquely national exercise.

8.4. Digital Platforms: The New Frontier of Free Speech and Censorship

Digital platforms such as social media websites, search engines, and online forums exist at the precipice of this struggle. They form the primary landscape where free speech is exercised and yet, where internet censorship can occur most prevalently. Their powers and responsibilities are ever-evolving within the tricky terrain of user rights, expression, regulation, and oversight.

Just as these platforms democratize the ease and reach of individual speech, they also manage, whether by choice or compliance, vast mechanisms of control and censorship. Content moderation policies, community standards, and algorithmic tweaks can often dictate the visibility, access, and impact of an individual's expression.

8.5. The Challenge Ahead: Constant Negotiation

Navigating the thin line between protecting free speech and enforcing internet censorship is and will continue to be an arduous journey. It requires constant negotiation, recalibration, and an understanding that the landscape is ever-evolving, influenced by technological advancements, shifting societal norms, and progressing legal interpretations.

Ultimately, prioritizing free speech and mitigating misuse via

censorship are not mutually exclusive goals. Both are imperative for constructing a digital world that respects individual freedoms while preserving the collective harmony and well-being inherent to our interconnected society. It's a pursuit that requires resolute attention, empathy, thoughtful deliberation, and most importantly, a ceaseless commitment to bettering our shared digital spaces.

Chapter 9. Lessons from Historical Social Media Lawsuits

Every corner of our increasingly digital world has been impacted by the sprawling influence of social media, not least of all our legal landscape, which has struggled to adapt its structures and regulations to accommodate the complexities of online behavior. The increasing number of lawsuits involving social media giants introduces a multitude of legal issues and challenges to existing frameworks, providing crucial insights into the landscape of rights, liabilities, and responsibilities painted on this unusual canvas.

9.1. Landmark Cases and their Implications

Let's begin by delving into some landmark cases which have profoundly impacted our perspectives on social media's role and influence in society.

In 2011, the case of Phonedog v. Noah Kravitz shone a spotlight on the value and ownership of social media followers. Kravitz, a former employee of Phonedog, a mobile news and reviews website, kept his Twitter account upon departing the company, along with its 17,000 followers. As a resolution to the ensuing corporate dispute, the case proposed the notion of placing monetary value on social media followers, prompting discussions on the commercial aspects of online presence and followership.

Continuing the trend of corporate conflicts, in 2015 Bland v. Roberts brought to fore the issue of employment termination based on interactions on social media platforms. Sheriff's Department employees in Virginia were fired for clicking the 'like' button on the Facebook page of their boss's electoral opponent. The Fourth Circuit court harbored the opinion that a Facebook 'like' constituted an expression of free speech, thus offering it legal protection. This gave rise to intensified debates on the interpretation and boundaries of virtual free speech.

One of the most notorious cases hogging the headlines more recently has been the Cambridge Analytica scandal, unfolding in 2018. Data of nearly 87 million Facebook users was harvested under the guise of academic research, only to be utilized for political advertising. This event cast a giant question mark over the safety of data privacy and protection in social media, leading to massive reforms in data governance and a heightened emphasis on user consent.

9.2. The Stakes of Social Media Defamation

Defamation, a concept traditionally rooted in print media, has migrated onto social media platforms as well, often with severe legal consequences.

In 2013, Elon Musk faced a defamation lawsuit for tweets allegedly damaging the reputation of a British caver involved in the Thai cave rescue operation. This episode highlighted the risks associated with impulsivity and lack of control exerted over expressions in the social media realm, even for high profile individuals.

Cases such as McAlpine v Bercow in 2013, UK, further illustrate this. Sally Bercow, the wife of the Speaker of the House of Commons, found herself in legal jeopardy for a seemingly innocent tweet linked to alleged child abuse. The case expanded the bounds of legally considered defamation to include insinuation and implications, not just overtly harmful statements.

9.3. Freedom of Speech Versus Online Harassment

The debate between maintaining freedom of speech and protecting users from online harassment is a perennial one in the legal world.

In the 2014 case, Elonis v. United States, Anthony Elonis was convicted for threats made against his wife on Facebook in the form of rap lyrics. He argued that his posts were a form of artistic expression protected by the First Amendment. However, the Supreme Court disagreed, making it clear that online threats, even in seemingly artistic forms, won't necessarily receive constitutional protection.

9.4. Data Ownership Disputes

Data ownership disputes are often at the core of social media lawsuits.

Likewise, in Fraley v. Facebook, users balked at the social networking giant using their images for 'Sponsored Stories' without explicit consent or compensation, eventually leading to a $20 million settlement. This case stressed the vital importance of clear and informed user consent when using their data for commercial practices.

These landmark cases have elicited an upheaval of the legal landscape in relation to social media, helping adapt longstanding legal doctrines to the digital age. The lessons from these historical social media lawsuits are pivotal to shaping our understanding of the expanding legal and ethical facets of social media. As we propel further into an digitally intertwined future, these lessons will serve as foundational guideposts to ensure safe, responsible, and respectful navigation of social media landscapes.

Chapter 10. Emerging Trends: New Laws and Ethical Challenges

The digital landscape continues to evolve as new technologies emerge and societal behaviors shift, thus spurring lawmakers and ethical watchdogs to constantly reassess and redefine the constructs that delineate appropriate actions within the realm of social media. The continuously changing nature of this digital platform necessitates ongoing adjustments and refinements to existing laws, as well as the introduction of novel regulations and discussions concerning ethical standards.

10.1. The Evolution of Legal Frameworks

Our journey into evolving trends begins with a glance over the morphing legal framework governing social media platforms. The bustling growth of these platforms has spurred regulators worldwide to revisit their governmental strategies, grappling with the challenge of governing a space that hosts a global audience but is not confined by geographical boundaries.

The California Consumer Privacy Act (CCPA) and the General Data Protection Regulation (GDPR) are standout models of modern legislation shaped to protect user privacy in a digital world. These regulations offer robust frameworks for consent and user data usage, painting the blueprint for regulatory shifts echoed worldwide. In India, the Personal Data Protection Bill (PDPB) and in Brazil, the General Data Protection Law (LGPD) have followed suit, reflecting international efforts in strengthening privacy norms.

However, privacy isn't the only issue; the emergence of deepfakes and misuse of Artificial Intelligence (AI) has thrown intellectual property laws into uncharted territories. Traditional laws struggle to handle the misuse of synthetic images and videos, leading to jurisdictional debates. These predicaments underline the necessity to continually update legal frameworks to match technological advancements.

10.2. The Ethical Dilemma: Balancing Rights and Responsibilities

Crossing the boundary from the legal sphere into the entity of ethics, the dynamism of emerging trends continues to challenge established norms. Our virtual presence extends far beyond being mere consumers; we are creators and contributors to the digital sphere, becoming custodians of information and technology.

The influence of AI algorithms on our consumption patterns has brought the ethical considerations of 'technological manipulation' to the fore. Behavioral nudging is not new, but AI-powered customizations open an ethical Pandora's box. The fine balance of using technology for enhancing the user experience while safeguarding against overreach is a pertinent ethical question.

Additionally, the social responsibility of platforms in disseminating news and handling misinformation remains a significant concern. The 'right to information' and 'freedom of expression' form the bedrock of democratic societies. However, the rampant spread of fake news during elections or a public health crisis like COVID-19 presents an ethical minefield. Platforms find themselves walking the tightrope between censorship and the responsible management of information.

10.3. Potential Legal and Ethical Responses

The unpredictable evolution of technology and social behavior demands flexibility and adaptability in our legal and ethical approaches. We are beginning to see legal responses to these challenges in the form of updated laws like the proposed Digital Services Act in the European Union, which aims to hold platforms accountable for content moderation.

From an ethical perspective, we see initiatives like the Santa Clara Principles on Transparency and Accountability in Content Moderation, an agreement that aims to instill increased transparency in how platforms handle and moderate content. Moreover, many social media companies have initiated external audits and public reports to create responsibility and establish trust.

As we grapple with the impact and influence of social media on our society, it is clear that we are at the forefront of a digital revolution, one that holds profound implications for the laws that bind us and the ethics that guide our behavior. By engaging in the rigorous examination of these emerging trends, we can hopeful promote a healthier, more mindful stewardship of social media, one that respects the rights and dignity of all participants within the digital sphere.

The final segment of this chapter illuminates the social media landscape, demonstrating that the world is in a state of constant motion. A continuous dialogue is required to keep abreast with changes in law, as well as ethical predicaments as they evolve. This engaging and lucid exploration of the laws and ethical norms that steer our digital actions will hopefully serve as a guide through the labyrinth of digital age jargon, legislation, and moral dilemmas.

Chapter 11. Shaping the Future: Responsible Social Media Practice

The digital realm of our interconnected society, of which social media is a significant part, has become an arena of sharp truths and blurry boundaries. As we move forward, it's crucial, now more than ever, to understand and navigate this terrain with responsibility. The use of social media should be steered by robust ethical considerations and adherence to privacy norms, data protection laws, and copyright stipulations.

11.1. A Vision for the Future of Social Media

Looking ahead, we must create an environment where social media can continue to provide value to users while ensuring their protection from potential harms. This means building a solid framework of ethical behavior and legal compliance, alongside fostering a culture of digital citizenship. Follower count and reach should not overshadow a commitment to truth, fairness, and respect for individuality.

By fostering a conscientious digital community, we can shape a future where the benefits of social media are enjoyed freely by all users. This includes ensuring that all voices are heard, opportunities are accessible to everyone, and that our collective digital footprint enriches rather than undermines society.

11.2. Responsible Social Media Practices for Individuals

For users, responsible social media use goes beyond simply adhering to platform terms and conditions. It involves awareness of the potential impact and repercussions of what we choose to share online. This means considering the context, potential harm or offense, and the wider ramifications of your posts. Honesty and authenticity should take center stage, while malicious behavior, false information, and disrespectful or harmful conduct should be decisively rejected.

Moreover, the safeguarding of personal data has never been so crucial. Users should exercise caution when sharing personal details online, ensure their accounts are secure, and be conscious of the attachments, links, and apps they interact with. Awareness of privacy settings, cookies, and data collection is a crucial part of this.

11.3. Adopting Ethical Business Behavior

For businesses, the responsible use of social media takes on an even more salient role. Accuracy of information, transparency in advertising and marketing, respect for consumer data privacy, and adherence to regulatory laws shouldn't be compromisable. While striving for user engagement and brand visibility, businesses must not lose sight of ethical considerations.

Furthermore, businesses should engage in responsible advertising, create spaces for fostering positive interactions, and disallow any form of harmful content on their platforms. They should also be ready to face and address any potential negative impact their social media activities could generate.

11.4. Anticipating and Managing Risks

In the realm of social media, risks can come from multiple points - misinformation, data breaches, cyberbullying, reputational damage. While each of these is distinct, they all demand proactive management. This could mean incorporating safeguards into platform design, using algorithms to track and manage harmful content or ensuring transparency and control over personal data. This demands not only improved technology, but also effective laws, and perhaps most importantly, an active, responsive community of users.

11.5. Engaging in Policy and Law Making

As we shape the future of social media, it's critical to be part of the ongoing conversation about how these platforms are governed. Users, platform operators, policymakers, and legal experts must work together to create robust and responsive regulations. This means clear guidelines on user rights, data privacy, content moderation, freedom of speech, as well as redressal mechanisms for conflicts.

In conclusion, shaping the future of responsible social media practice calls for a collective effort. We must forge a path that not only harnesses the potentials of these platforms but also mitigates their risks. Through thoughtful engagement, guided by a strong framework of laws and ethical practices, we can create a better and safer digital world for us all.